INTRODUCTION

On 4 February 1818, a distinguished group of men gathered on the stair outside the Crown Room in Edinburgh Castle. Standing beside the Lord President of the Court of Session, the Lord Justice Clerk, the Lord Chief Commissioner of the Jury Court, the Lord Provost of the City of Edinburgh and the Commander-in-Chief of the Army was an anxious Walter Scott, one of Scotland's foremost authors and antiquarians. His urgent pleas to the Prince Regent (the future King George IV) had resulted in a Royal Warrant permitting Scott to accompany the Scottish Officers of State to open the sealed Crown Room in search of the Scottish Crown, Sceptre and Sword of State, known as the Honours of Scotland.

The group watched in silence as the masonry blocking was removed from the doorway. In the darkness beyond they spied a great iron-bound oak chest. They approached with great apprehension, for there was a suspicion that the chest was empty. The Honours had been locked away in 1707 following the Treaty of Union with England but many believed that ceremony was a hoax.

Let Walter Scott himself describe what then happened:

"The chest seemed to return a hollow and empty sound to the strokes of the hammer, and even those whose expectations had been most sanguine felt at the moment the probability of disappointment…The joy was therefore extreme when, the ponderous lid of the chest being forced open, the Regalia were discovered lying at the bottom covered with linen cloths, exactly as they had been left in the year 1707…The reliques were passed from hand to hand, and greeted with the affectionate reverence which emblems so venerable, restored to public view after the slumber of more than a hundred years, were so peculiarly calculated to excite. The discovery was instantly communicated to the public by the display of the Royal Standard, and was greeted by shouts of the

soldiers in the garrison, and a vast multitude assembled on the Castle Hill; indeed the rejoicing was so general and sincere as plainly to show that, however altered in other respects, the people of Scotland had lost nothing of that national enthusiasm which formerly had displayed itself in grief for the loss of these emblematic Honours, and now was expressed in joy for their recovery."

No-one can have been more overjoyed than the "Wizard of the North" himself. And the drama of that February morning proved a fitting climax to the fascinating and eventful story of the Honours of the Kingdom, a story which begins in the Dark Ages and takes us through the glory of Scotland's medieval history.

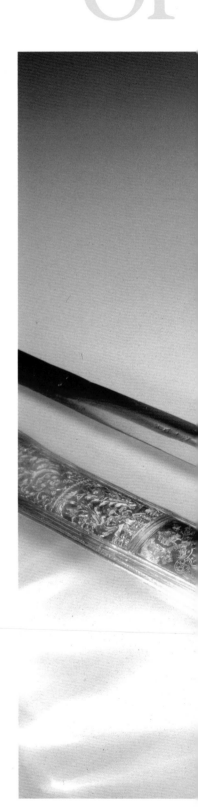

Honours the Kingdom

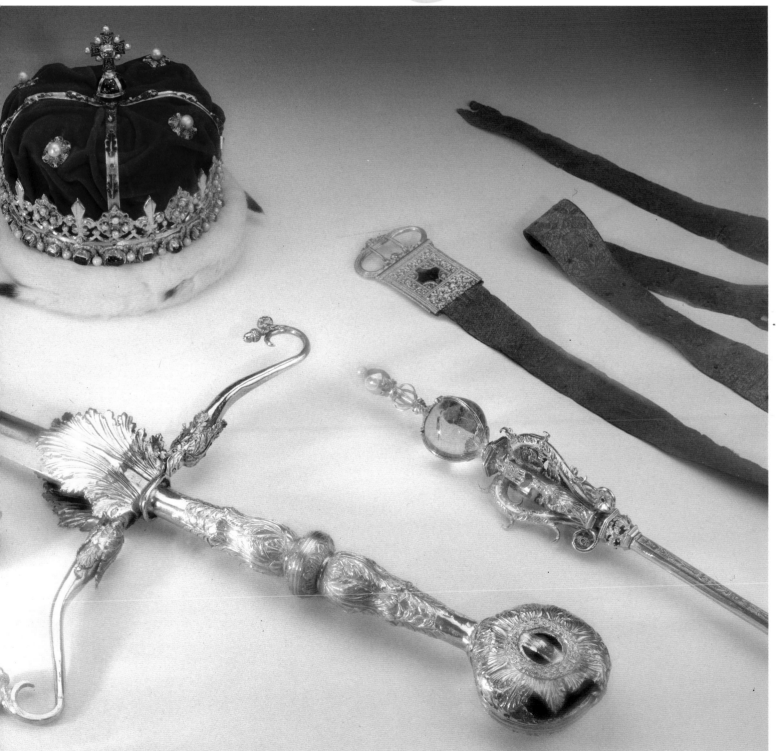

Scotland

SCONE PALACE
FROM ACROSS THE
RIVER TAY

SCONE, TRADITIONALLY THE PLACE OF INAUGURATION OF THE PICTISH
KINGS OF FORTRIU IN THE SEVENTH CENTURY AND OF THE KINGS OF
SCOTS WHO SUCCEEDED THEM AFTER 842.

SCONE, "WHERE THE SALT WATERS OF THE SEA (AND THE POWERS OF
DEATH WHO DWELL IN THEM) ARE FINALLY TURNED BACK BY THE
LIVING WATERS OF THE RIVER. SCONE 'OF THE HIGH SHIELDS', 'OF
MELODIOUS SHIELDS', AS THE ELEVENTH-CENTURY PROPHECY OF
BERCHÁN CALLED IT, REFERRING SURELY TO THE CLASH OF SHIELDS AT
THE ACCLAMATION OF A NEW KING."

(A.DUNCAN SCOTLAND: THE MAKING OF THE KINGDOM)

On New Year's Day in the year 1651,
Charles II was crowned King of Scots in the
tiny church beside Scone Palace by Perth.
It proved to be the last Coronation there,
and indeed the last in Scotland.

Many a king before Charles had been
enthroned at Scone, traditionally the place of
inauguration of Pictish Kings since at least the
seventh century. A glittering array of monarchs,
including Macbeth, Malcolm Canmore,
John Balliol and Robert the Bruce, had all
journeyed to the ancient mound, the Moot Hill,
to declare publicly their acceptance of the
rights and obligations of kingship, to receive
the symbols of sovereignty and accept the
homage of their loyal subjects.

On that Ne'er Day in 1651, the young
Charles II was mantled in royal robes and
presented with the "Honores of Scotland", the
Crown, Sceptre and Sword, together with a pair
of Spurs. These are the Honours of Scotland
which are today displayed in the Crown Room
in Edinburgh Castle. They date from the reign
of King James IV (1488-1513) and his son
King James V (1513-42). But how old is the
tradition whereby the monarch achieved
sovereignty only upon accepting the symbols of
power, the Crown, the Sceptre and the Sword?

THE RIVER TAY BENDING

AT TREE-CLAD SCONE,

VIEWED FROM KINNOULL

HILL BY PERTH

THE MOOT HILL, SCONE.

THE PRESENT BUILDING UPON THE LOW

MOUND IS THE MAUSOLEUM OF THE

EARLS OF MANSFIELD WHICH REPLACES

THE EARLIER CHURCH WHERE

KING CHARLES II WAS CROWNED

SUNSET OVER IONA FROM THE COAST OF MULL

ST COLUMBA'S WINDOW
IN ST MARGARET'S CHAPEL,
EDINBURGH CASTLE

IONA, "THE ISLAND OF IO", THE TINY SPECK OF LAND IN THE WESTERN SEA

WHERE THE HOLY MAN OF GOD COLUMBA - COLUM CILLE, "DOVE OF THE CHURCH" - MADE HIS

HOME AND IN SO DOING CREATED THE SPIRITUAL HOME OF CHRISTIANITY.

IONA, WHERE THE FIRST KINGS OF SCOTS WERE ORDAINED AND WHERE MANY OF THEM WERE

FINALLY LAID TO REST. SHORTLY BEFORE COLUM CILLE HIMSELF PASSED AWAY, ABOUT THE

YEAR 586, HE STOOD UPON A HILL OVERLOOKING HIS BLESSED CHURCH

AND UTTERED THESE WORDS:

"ON THIS PLACE, SMALL AND MEAN THOUGH IT BE, NOT ONLY THE KINGS OF SCOTS WITH

THEIR PEOPLES, BUT ALSO THE RULERS OF BARBAROUS AND FOREIGN NATIONS,

WITH THEIR SUBJECTS, WILL BESTOW GREAT AND ESPECIAL HONOUR."

THE ANCIENT KINGS OF SCOTS AND THE SYMBOLS OF SOVEREIGN POWER

In 574, it is written, an angel appeared to Saint Columba, Abbot of Iona, and commanded him to ordain Áedán mac Gabhráin King of the Scots of Dál Riata. According to Adomnán, Columba's biographer:

"The saint, in obedience to the command of the Lord, sailed across to the island of Io (Iona), and there ordained, as he had been commanded, Áedán to be King, who had arrived at the same time as the saint. During the words of consecration, the saint declared the future regarding the children, grandchildren and great-grandchildren of Áedán, and laying his hand upon his head, he ordained and blessed him."

This is the first tantalising glimpse we have of the inauguration ceremony of a Scottish king. There is no mention either of crowning or of anointment; just the simple act of ordination, the "laying on of hands", by the holy man Columba.

A further clue to the nature of the ceremony is given by Cumméne the White, the seventh Abbot of Iona, who recorded that the saint began to prophesy by saying to King Áedán:

"Charge your sons that they also shall charge their sons and grandsons and descendants, not through evil counsels to lose their sceptre of this kingdom from their hands."

THE ABBEY OF IONA

DUNADD, THE ROCKY FORTRESS RISING FROM THE BROAD FLOOD PLAIN OF
MOINE MHÒR 'THE GREAT MOSS'.
DARK-AGE DUNADD, THE "CHIEF PLACE OF THE DISTRICT" AND ROYAL RESIDENCE OF
THE KINGS OF THE SCOTS OF DÀL RIATA.
MIGHT THE INTRIGUING CARVINGS NEAR ITS SADDLE-BACKED SUMMIT -
THE FOOTPRINTS AND THE BASIN HOLLOWED OUT OF THE LIVING ROCK -HAVE BEEN
LINKED IN SOME WAY TO THE INAUGURATION OF THESE ANCIENT KINGS?

THE BASIN   THE FOOTPRINTS

In Dark-Age Scotland, as elsewhere in Europe, kings like Áedán, who ruled over a people recently arrived from Ireland, and the kings of the native-born Picts, were more like tribal warlords who exacted tribute from the peoples in their territory and led raiding parties beyond it. But through the Middle Ages, the nature of kingship changed. As the nations of Europe emerged, along with the Christian-isation of the West, the Sceptre and Sword were fixed as instruments of sovereignty.

The Sceptre signified the sacred nature of kingship, bestowing an authority to rule with discretion and sincerity, not with tyranny and partiality. The Sword, on the other hand, was a symbol of power on earth, imposing on its holder a duty both to dispense justice and to protect his subjects from their enemies.

About 842, Kenneth mac Alpin, already King of the Scots, became King of the Picts. Thus the nature of kingship changed. The Scottish royal house was transformed from a remote Irish warband, perched on its rocky fortresses at Dunadd and elsewhere, into a powerful dynasty controlling a greater part of northern Britain from its base at Scone.

Sadly, no regalia have survived from early medieval Scotland and we have to wait until the thirteenth century for further information about the inauguration of the medieval Kings of Scots.

In his *Chronicle*, John of Fordun details the events of the summer's day in 1249 when King Alexander III was enthroned at Scone:

"A great many nobles led Alexander up to the cross which stands in the graveyard, at the east end of the church. There they set him on the royal throne, which was decked with silken cloths inwoven with gold; and the Bishop of St Andrews consecrated him King. So the King sat down upon the royal throne - that is, the stone - while the earls and other nobles, on bended knee, strewed their garments under his feet before the stone.

Now this stone is reverently kept in that monastery, for the consecration of the Kings of Alba [the ancient name for Scotland]; and no King was ever wont to reign in Scotland, unless he had first, on receiving the name of King, sat upon this stone of Scone.

But lo! when all was over, a Highland Scot suddenly fell on his knee before the throne and, bowing his head, hailed the King in his mother tongue [that is, Gaelic] and recited, even unto the end, the pedigree of the Kings of Scots."

The ceremony was closer to the inauguration of a pagan chieftain than to a Christian coronation. It was held in the open air; the central act was the setting of the King on a stone, symbolic of his union with the land and its people; allegiance was rendered to the new King; and a Highland bard recited the King's genealogy.

Fordun makes no mention of King Alexander III being crowned or invested with other emblems of kingship. But it may be that he was wearing a Crown on that July day and carrying a Sceptre. On a seal of Scone Abbey, which appears to depict his Inauguration, the youthful King is enthroned with an open lily Crown on his head and a Sceptre in his right hand.

11

EARLY SYMBOLS OF SOVEREIGNTY

The earliest representation of a Scottish king bearing his symbols of sovereign power is 150 years earlier than Alexander's reign, on a royal seal of Edgar. The King is wearing a Crown and carrying a Sceptre and Sword. On a seal of his successor, King Alexander I, there is the Orb,

KING EDGAR'S SEAL.

signifying the sacred nature of kingship. In a miniature painting from a charter to Kelso Abbey, dated 1159, depicting Alexander's younger brother, David I, and David's grandson, Malcolm IV ("The Maiden"), both Kings are shown crowned, with David holding a Sword and Orb and Malcolm a Sword and Sceptre. An orb never became one of the pieces of Scottish Royal Regalia in succeeding reigns.

KING DAVID I AND HIS GRANDSON, KING MALCOLM IV

Why did Fordun not mention the presence of these symbols in 1249, when they obviously existed? Presumably because they were only an incidental part of the ceremony. But by the thirteenth century the Scottish Kings were attaching far greater importance to the Christian rites of coronation and anointment practised on the Continent and were determined to give them a central place in the "kingmaking" ceremony. This was a perfectly understandable concern. A king not dignified by these Christian emblems and rites at his enthronement was not considered fully a sovereign king.

King Alexander II made several appeals to the Pope for the privilege of Kings of Scots to be crowned and anointed. All were rejected following representations by the English King Henry III, who was determined to limit the authority of the Kings of Scots. An important breakthrough came in 1251, two years after Alexander III's inauguration, when Pope Innocent IV finally refused King Henry's submission that English agreement had to be obtained before Kings of Scots could be

anointed and crowned. It was to be a further seventy-eight years, however, before full Papal recognition would be granted.

The first written record of the Crown and other Royal Regalia occurs at the close of the short and ill-starred reign of John Balliol (1292-96). In a little under four years this luckless monarch, placed on the throne as a vassal of the English King Edward I, had lost his Crown, and all the trappings of kingship. His reign came to an end in 1296 in a humiliating ceremony held at Montrose Castle before the English King. The chronicler, Andrew of Wyntoun, described the spectacle:

"This Iohun the Balliol dispoyilzeide he
Off al his robis of ryalte.
The pellour thai tuk out of his tabart,
Twme Tabart he was callit eftirwart;
And al vthire insignyis
That fel to kynge on ony wise,
Baythe septure, suerde, crowne and rynge,
Fra this Iohun, that he made kynge,
Hallely fra hym he tuk thare,
And mad hym of his kynrik bare."

"This John of Balliol deprived he
Of all his robes of royalty.
The fur they took out of his tabard (coat),
Empty Coat he was called afterwards;
And all other insignia
That fell to king in any way,
Both sceptre, sword, crown and ring,
From this John, that he made king,
Wholly from him he took there,
And made him of his kingdom bare."

of the BALIOUN

The Sceptre, Sword, Crown and Ring
removed that day from King John did not stay
long in Scotland. They were taken almost
immediately to England along with the other
treasures looted from the royal castles.
One other powerful symbol of Scottish
kingship - the great Stone of Scone on which
the kings were set at their enthronement - was
taken south to England with the Honours
of Scotland.

"And then in haste to Scone rode he,
And there was crowned without delay
All in the manner of that day,
And on the royal throne was set."

(The Inauguration of King Robert I in 1306,
from John Barbour's The Bruce)

KING ROBERT THE BRUCE AND THE CIRCLET OF GOLD

When Robert the Bruce seized the throne of Scotland in 1306, both the Stone of Scone and the Honours were well beyond his grasp. But new symbols of sovereignty could be easily fashioned. Bruce duly journeyed to the ancient Moot Hill of Scone in the Spring of that year, to be set upon his throne on Lady Day, Friday 25 March. A hastily-made circlet of gold was placed upon the King's head. Two days later, on Palm Sunday, the newly-crowned King attended a High Mass in the abbey church there. As Christ had entered Jerusalem, so King Robert now entered his Kingdom.

No sooner had he done so than he was forced to leave it. Within three months of the ceremony at Scone, his army was routed in battle near Methven and Bruce fled west to escape the wrath of King Edward of England. Such was the confusion that the newly-made golden circlet fell into English hands once more and it was taken south to England. There is no record that it was ever returned and the legend that Bruce's circlet of gold forms part of the present Crown must be false.

King Robert must surely have commanded that new Honours be made following his thunderous victory over the English at Bannockburn in June 1314: such was the importance he attached to "the honours which go with the rule of the realm of Scotland". Fifteen years later, as the elderly King lay dying at his manor at Cardross, on the northern shore of the Firth of Clyde, his ambasssador, Master Alexander Kinninmonth, at last won the consent of the Pope to the crowning and anointing of the Scottish kings. The Papal Bull, issued just six days after King Robert had died, was final recognition by Christendom's highest authority of the independence of the Scottish kingdom. The crowning, which for so long had played a secondary part in the inauguration of her kings, was now pre-eminent.

With King Robert dead, the Scots soon exercised their right of crowning and anointing a new king. Bruce's only son, David, at the tender age of five, was duly enthroned at

Scone on 24 November 1331. By all accounts it was a ceremony of great and solemn splendour, with no expense spared. A special Sceptre was made to fit the young King's hands. According to John of Fordun, David was:

"...anointed King of Scotland, and crowned, by the Lord James Bennet, Bishop of St Andrews, specially appointed thereunto by a Bull of the most holy father John XXII. We do not read that any of the Kings of Scotland, before this David, were anointed, or with such solemnity crowned."

The Coronation of King David II confirmed Scotland's status as a truly independent nation, her sovereign answerable to no-one but the Holy Father. The Crown, Sword of State, and Sceptre received by the King on that November day were the visible manifestation of that independence.

It is assumed that these same symbols of sovereign power were presented to King David II's successor, King Robert II (the first sovereign of the Royal House of Stewart) and to his successors until the reign of King James IV, who ascended the throne in 1488. But what became of these ancient Regalia, last used at King James IV's Coronation, remains a mystery. During King James's reign and that of his son, King James V, they were replaced by the Honours that are now on display in the Crown Room in Edinburgh Castle.

T H E Honours

KING JAMES IV AND THE PAPAL GIFTS

The slim Sceptre with its elaborate finial and the awesome Sword of State were created in the warm climes of Renaissance Italy by craftsmen working for the Supreme Pontiff of the Christian world - the Pope in Rome. Papal support had been vital to the sovereigns of Scotland in the prolonged Wars of Independence when England had sought to dominate its poorer northern neighbour. One result of pontifical support was the special status of Scotland as a "special daughter" of the Holy See.

THE SCEPTRE AS GIVEN BY POPE ALEXANDER VI, WITH THE SWORD OF STATE

A GOLDEN ROSE GIVEN BY POPE PIUS II TO THE REPUBLIC OF SIENA IN 1459

KING JAMES III AT PRAYER, ABOUT 1471

The exchange of gifts was an important and integral part of political life in the Middle Ages. Any papal gift to a European monarch had immense prestige and religious significance. One such gift was the Golden Rose.

This was in the form of a cluster of roses mounted on a stem attached to a pedestal base. Flowers and leaves were of pure gold. The largest flower was set with a precious stone of reddish hue, such as an amethyst, and also had a receptacle for balsam and musk to give fragrance to the rose. The Golden Rose conveyed a spiritual message and was a symbol of papal esteem for the recipient.

THE HEAD
OF THE
SCEPTRE

On 5 March 1486 Pope Innocent VIII announced that James III King of Scots would be presented with the Golden Rose. This was a singular honour to the sovereign of a small realm beyond the mainland of Europe. The last papal gift to Scotland had been made three centuries before when King William the Lion received the Golden Rose from Pope Lucius II in 1182. During May 1486, the papal legate Giacomo Passarella, Bishop of Imola, delivered the Rose itself to King James. It was to be the first of a remarkable series of gifts from the Popes.

King James III was succeeded by his son James in 1488. Despite the part played by the latter in the downfall of his father, it did not alter the benevolence of Pope Innocent VIII who repeated the gift of a Golden Rose to the new King of Scots in 1491. Unfortunately neither of the Roses has survived the vagaries of Scottish history.

It is possible that the silver-gilt Sceptre, the earliest of the Scottish papal gifts to survive, was presented to King James IV at the same time as the Golden Rose. But tradition has it that the Sceptre was a gift in 1494 from Pope Alexander VI, who succeeded Innocent VIII.

In 1502, to complement the Sceptre, King James IV ordered a Sword of Honour, with a scabbard, from the Edinburgh cutler Robert Selkirk. This was carried by the crowned King, also holding his papal Sceptre, the following year at a meeting of the Parliament. However, the native-made Sword was soon superseded by yet another munificent papal gift to the King, this time from Pope Julius II. He was the "Warrior Pope", who commissioned the artist Michelangelo to paint the ceiling of the Sistine Chapel in Rome. The Pope actually presented two gifts: a Blessed Sword and a Consecrated Hat. These were formally handed to the King during a solemn High Mass on Easter Sunday 1507 in the Gothic splendour of the abbey church of Holyrood. The papal envoy was an Italian knight named Antonio Inviziati. He had set out from Italy in December 1506 accompanied by his suite and arrived in Scotland on 31 March 1507. King James was very conscious of the honour accorded him and sent a fulsome letter of gratitude to the Pope.

POPE JULIUS II

THE PROCESSIONAL DOORWAY THROUGH THE WEST FRONT OF HOLYROOD ABBEY

The Sword and Scabbard were made by Domenico da Sutri. They were created in the period of the so-called High Renaissance and their sumptuous appearance reflects the decorative style then in vogue in Italy. Da Sutri took the Arms of Pope Julius as the theme for the decoration of the Sword handle, scabbard and belt. The oak tree and acorns, symbols of the Risen Christ, plus the dolphins, symbolic of Christ's Church, form part of an imaginative and meaningful ornamentation whose quality exceeds that on the Crown and Sceptre.

THE SWORD OF STATE SHEATHED

Two other swords made by da Sutri as papal gifts have survived. They are very similar in appearance to the Scottish Sword of State. One was presented to King Ladislaus II of Hungary in 1509 and, because it is in a better state of preservation, indicates what has been lost from the Scottish Sword. The buckle holes on the belt, for example, are reinforced by small silver-gilt sprays of oak leaves and acorns. The second sword, a gift to the Swiss Cantons in 1511, has lost part of one dolphin quillon. Both scabbards are undamaged.

The Consecrated Hat presented to King James IV with the Sword has not survived. Extant examples from the sixteenth century are made of dark crimson velvet, lined with ermine. They have a stiff high crown surrounded by a deep brim which curves upwards to a point at the front. There are two lappets (ornamental ribbons) hanging down from the back. On the right-hand side of the Hat an embroidered gold dove, decorated with pearls, symbolises the Holy Spirit. From the top of the crown alternate straight and wavy rays, outlined in gold thread and filled with seed pearls, descend towards the brim.

THE SWORD OF STATE

The steel blade of the Sword is 991mm long and 44mm wide at its broadest part. Near the hilt the blade is etched on each side. One side has the figure of St Peter, the other St Paul. Beneath each are etched the words: JULIUS II PONT MAX ...(Julius II Supreme Pontiff...). The etched lines of the figures and lettering were originally inlaid with gold.

The silver-gilt handle for the blade is 387mm long with dolphin-shaped quillons having a total width of 438mm. The handle was all of repoussé work but at some stage the dolphins have been cast from the originals and replaced, possibly by the goldsmith Matthew Auchinleck in 1516. The handle above the quillons is decorated with oak leaves and acorns and terminates in a circular pommel which once had inset enamelled plates. At the bottom of the handle are two stylised oak leaves (broken at the points) which overlap the scabbard at its mouth.

THE SCABBARD

The scabbard is 1128mm long and 50mm wide. It is made of wood, covered in dark red velvet, and mounted with silver-gilt repoussé work. On the front of the scabbard at the mouth is an enamelled panel bearing the Arms of Pope Julius II: Azure an oak tree eradicated and fructed Or. Above the Arms is the symbol of the Papacy - crossed keys linked by a tasseled cord surmounted by the papal tiara. The remaining length of the scabbard is divided into three areas by two circles which once held enamelled plates.

The three areas are filled with elaborate decoration (missing in places) of oak leaves, acorns, dolphins, and grotesque masks. This form of ornament is repeated on the reverse of the scabbard though sections are missing. There are fittings for the sword belt on the reverse near the mouth of the scabbard.

THE HILT OF THE

SWORD OF STATE

THE ENAMELLED ARMS

OF POPE JULIUS II AND

THE SILVER-GILT

REPOUSSÉ DETAIL ON

THE SCABBARD

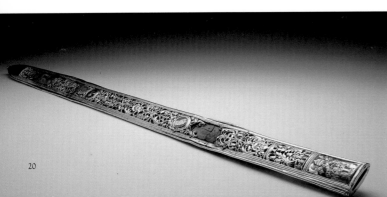

THE SWORD BELT

The sword belt is 1499mm long. It is
of woven silk and gold thread featuring the
personal Arms of Pope Julius repeated along the
whole length, each shield shape being linked to
the next with leafy ornament. The belt is
fastened by a massive silver-gilt buckle with
hinged prongs.

KING JAMES V AND THE SCEPTRE

King James IV was killed fighting the forces of Henry VIII of England at the Battle of Flodden in 1513. His heir was an infant son and Scotland was governed by a Regent until 1524. King James V, aged sixteen, finally took power into his own hands in 1528. European politics at the time placed James V in a position where his favours were sought by the Pope, the Emperor, and the Kings of France and England. Conscious of his kingly prestige James sought to enhance the symbols of his sovereignty - the Sceptre and the Crown. He began with the Sceptre.

In 1536 the Edinburgh goldsmith Adam Leys remodelled the Sceptre and added to its length. When presented to King James IV, the Sceptre had consisted of a handle attached to a hexagonal rod with a finial incorporating a ball of rock crystal. Leys appears to have taken moulds of the Italian-made finial and cast the work anew in solid silver, adding another section to the hexagonal shaft. The extra length makes the appearance of the Sceptre instantly more impressive.

This, the earliest surviving papal gift, now consists of the original handle attached to a hexagonal rod, engraved on three of its six sides with urns, leaves, and grotesque masks. A knop divides the original pieces from the new section which is also hexagonal. This has been engraved with thistles and fleurs de lis with the King's initials (IR5 for Jacobus Rex V) engraved at the top of the rod.

The finial is flanked by stylised dolphins with tails curling round applied flower shapes.

Between the dolphins are three small figures, each under a Gothic canopy.

The first figure is the Virgin, crowned with an open crown, holding the naked Child on her right arm. She carries an orb in her left hand. To the left of the Virgin and Child is St James with a book in his right hand and a staff in his left. This has been broken, and the top is missing. Damage has also occurred to the third figure, St Andrew, patron and protector of Scotland. He holds an open book in his left hand; with his right he grasps a saltire cross which has lost the upper two arms.

Above this group is a polished globe of rock crystal, a substance believed in the Middle Ages to have mystical properties. The crystal is kept in place by three silver strips which come together at the top to support a pierced knop. The finial terminates with another small golden globe surmounted by a pearl.

THE HEAD OF THE SCEPTRE

WITH ITS CRYSTAL GLOBE

THE SCEPTRE

TRANSFORMED

DETAILS FROM THE

ORIGINAL (LEFT)

AND NEW PORTIONS

OF THE ROD

22

LEFT TO RIGHT –

ST ANDREW,

THE VIRGIN AND CHILD,

ST JAMES

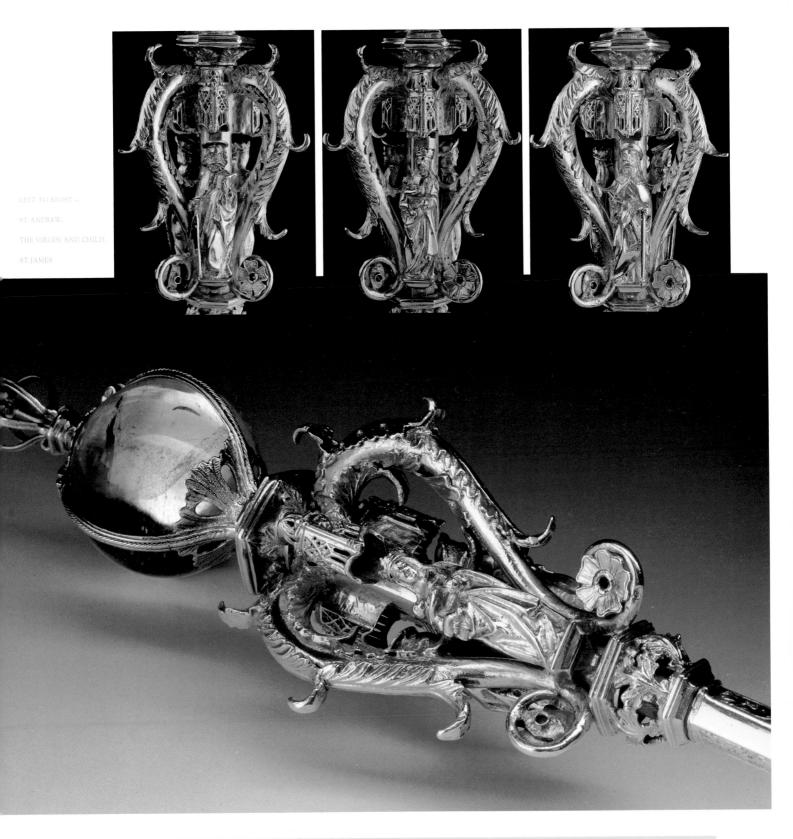

LEFT TO RIGHT –
ST ANDREW,
THE VIRGIN AND CHILD,
ST JAMES

THE HONOURS AND THE ROYAL ARMS
OF SCOTLAND

One small, but important, consequence of enhancing the Sceptre was a change in the Royal Arms of Scotland. Part of the Arms is the crest, which is located on top of the helmet above the shield. From about 1502, the Scottish crest consisted of a seated crowned lion holding a sword in one paw and a flag in the other. At the time the Sceptre was lengthened, the saltire flag on the crest was replaced with a sceptre. This change allows the crest lion to hold two of the Honours of Scotland - the Sword and Sceptre - and to wear the third, the Crown. Thus representations of the Regalia became part of the Royal Arms of Scotland.

KING JAMES V
AND THE CROWN
OF SCOTLAND

At the end of 1536, King James V sailed to the Continent where he married Princess Madeleine, daughter of Francis I, King of France. The marriage took place on 1 January 1537 in the Cathedral of Notre Dame in Paris. The royal couple remained in France until May. While at Compiègne on 19 February, James was presented with a Blessed Sword and Consecrated Hat from the papal legate acting for Pope Paul III. Although these additional examples of papal favour were carried back to Scotland, neither has survived.

Sadly, Madeleine died within seven weeks of her arrival in Scotland and before she could be crowned Queen. James quickly found a new French bride and married Mary of Guise-Lorraine in 1538. The Coronation of Queen Mary in February 1540 provided the King with the opportunity to consider the condition of his own Crown.

We can only speculate on the shape of the Crown inherited by King James V. From the reign of King Edgar (1097-1107) to the reign of King James II (1437-60) the Crown of Scotland is shown as a circular fillet with a varying number of fleurs de lis round the rim.

The first evidence for a change of shape appears on a silver coin struck in 1484 during the reign of King James III. The coin is a groat bearing a portrait of the monarch wearing his Crown. The royal diadem consists of a fillet with eight fleurs de lis having four arches surmounted by an orb and cross. This form of Crown is described as imperial. Several monarchs of ancient independent European kingdoms adopted the arched crown towards the end of the fifteenth century.

The earliest illustration of King James IV wearing an imperial Crown is in the *Book of Hours* made for the King to commemorate his marriage to Margaret Tudor in 1503. The Crown has eight larger fleurs de lis with alternate smaller fleurs de lis or crosses. There are four arches, each decorated with four applied ornaments, surmounted by a small orb and cross. The Crown appears to be set with precious stones and pearls. The general appearance is delicate, suggesting that it does not contain a great mass of gold.

Presumably this was an accurate portrayal of the Crown worn by King James IV. The Treasurer's accounts show that it was repaired by Matthew Auchinleck in 1503, possibly because it was light and delicate. The Crown had to be repaired again in 1532, this time by the goldsmith Thomas Wood. By the time an inventory of royal jewels was made in March 1539, further damage had been done. The Crown is described as having one fleur de lis broken off and lost. The inventory gives the weight of the Crown as 16ozs 15dwt Scots. The condition of the Crown obviously did not satisfy King James V and he ordered major changes to the principal symbol of kingship.

The goldsmith appointed to undertake the work was John Mosman, a member of the Incorporation of Goldsmiths in Edinburgh.

CRAWFORD MOOR IN CLYDESDALE,
"GOD'S TREASURE-HOUSE IN SCOTLAND".
CRAWFORD MOOR, WHERE "GOLD IS YET FOUND
BY PASSING THE EARTH THROUGH SEARCHES,
AND THE SAME BROUGHT DOWN WITH SPEATS [SPATES] OF RAINE.
I HAVE SEEN PIECES OF IT AS BIG AS A CHERRY.
IT IS EXCEEDING FINE GOLD".

(COLONEL BORTHWICK, MINES DIRECTOR, 1684)

"HERE MOUNTAINS RAISE THEIR HEATH'RY BANKS,
RANGED HUGE ABOON THE LIFT,
IN WHASE DARK BOWELS, FOR LEAD TRACTS,
SWARMED MINERS HOWK AND SIFT.
A WIMPLAN [WANDERING] BURN ATWEEN THE HILLS,
THRO' MONY A GLEN RINS TROTTIN';
AMANG THE STANES AN' SUNNY RILLS
AFT BITS OF GOWD [GOLD] ARE GOTTEN;"

(FROM ALEXANDER WILSON'S
EPISTLE TO WILLIAM MITCHELL
WRITTEN AT LEADHILLS 1790)

Mosman had been commissioned in 1539 to make the Queen's Crown. Now in January of 1540 he set about refashioning the Crown of Scotland. His craftsmanship is typical of Scottish work at the time, lacking the fine skill shown by the best contemporary Continental goldsmiths.

Apart from receiving the damaged Crown, Mosman was also given from the Mint forty-one ounces of gold which had been mined at Crawford Moor in Upper Clydesdale. He was also paid for twenty-three precious stones to add to the twenty gemstones and sixty-eight pearls in the broken Crown. Among the new stones were three large garnets and a large amethyst. Mosman was also given a new orb and cross to fix on top of the arches.

With that extra gold, new stones and finial Mosman set about remodelling the Crown. Both the sequence of construction and the new work undertaken by him can be deduced from the Crown itself.

REVERSE OF THE

FRENCH FINIAL

SHOWING THE

INITIALS OF

KING JAMES V

John Mosman started by dismantling the four arches from the broken Crown, then carefully removing the existing stones and pearls. He melted down the remaining circlet and added the extra forty-one ounces of Scottish gold. He then cast ten fleurs de lis and ten crosses fleury before making a broad flat band edged top and bottom with a decorative strip. The band was then formed into an oval and soldered together to form the basic circlet.

Mosman attached an undulating ring of forty gold half circles to the top edge of the circlet. This ring carries the ten alternate fleurs de lis and crosses fleury, each separated by a pearl. The crosses fleury are enriched by four pearls surrounding a central transparent gemstone. The twenty precious stones from the old Crown are either circular, square, triangular, or lozenge-shaped. They were set below the fleurs de lis and crosses. The twenty-two new stones are of varied shape and size but he placed them in individual claw settings. These are contained within ovoid rectangular frames with leaf-shaped sides and enamelled top and bottom sections. The frames were individually made and attached to the circlet. Between the enamelled settings are twenty-two large oriental pearls. The circlet and its decoration are all new work by John Mosman.

To the circlet he added the four arches from the old Crown, each decorated with three gold and red-enamelled oak leaves (two are replacements). At the point where the arches meet there is an ornament of four chased gold leaves, which are the base for the orb and cross. King James may have brought the orb from Paris in 1537 as the workmanship is French. The orb is made of gold, enamelled blue, and spangled with small stars which have been left uncoloured. Horizontal and vertical bands enclose the upper part of the orb and at one time four jewels hung from the horizontal band. Above the orb is a gold cross with leafy ornament on the arms, set off with black enamel. In the centre of the cross at the front is the large amethyst acquired by Mosman. At the foot of the cross on the back is a small rectangular panel with the letters IR5 for Jacobus Rex V. The cross is enhanced with eight oriental pearls held in place with small gold rosettes.

ONE OF THE

FOUR BONNET

ORNAMENTS

To complete the Crown, King James ordered a purple velvet bonnet lined with purple satin. The old Crown had a bonnet from at least 1503 which was renewed in 1532. The new bonnet was tailored by Thomas Arthur of Edinburgh who charged 5/- for manufacture and £3 12s 6d for the materials. Mosman drilled four pairs of small holes on the lower moulding of the circlet to enable the bonnet to be stitched to the Crown. (The bonnet has been replaced on several occasions. King James VII ordered that the colour of the bonnet be changed to red. The present bonnet was made in 1993).

The final touch of richness is given by four delicate ornaments, adorned with an oriental pearl set on a pierced oblong of gold, all enamelled in red, blue, green and white. These are attached to the bonnet between the four arches.

FLEUR DE LIS · ARCH · CROSS FLEURY

THE COMPONENTS
OF THE CIRCLET

DIAMONDS
ON

ENAMELLED

DECORATIVE

SETTING

STRIP

LARGE

GEMSTONE

When the refashioned Crown of
Scotland was complete it weighed 3lb 10oz and
Mosman arranged for John Paterson to make a
box to hold it. On 13 February 1540 the new
Crown was delivered to the King at the Palace
of Holyroodhouse, by now the favoured
residence of the royal family in Edinburgh.
King James wore it for the first time at his
Consort's Coronation nine days later, in the
abbey church of Holyrood.

Queen Mary, The Honours

MARY QUEEN
OF SCOTS

THE CORONATION OF MARY QUEEN OF SCOTS

King James V died on 14 December 1542 at Falkland Palace, in Fife, at the early age of thirty. Just six days earlier his second Queen, Mary of Guise-Lorraine, had given birth to a baby girl in the royal palace at Linlithgow. She was named Mary after her mother.

Scotland was at war with England and, for the child's safety, she was moved to the secure refuge of Stirling Castle. On Sunday 9 September 1543, the nine-month-old infant was wrapped in the Royal Robes and carried in solemn procession from the Palace across the courtyard and into the Chapel Royal. There she was crowned Queen of Scots. The Honours were taken to Stirling for the occasion and the new Crown was used for the first time at the Coronation of a sovereign of Scotland. Indeed, the three Honours we see today were first used together at Mary's crowning.

It must surely have been the most moving of occasions in view of Mary's tender age. As Governor of Scotland, the Earl of Arran bore the Crown; the Earl of Lennox, later to be Mary's father-in-law, bore the Sceptre. Cardinal Beaton consecrated the little Queen, placing the Crown upon her infant brow, the Sceptre in her tiny hand, and girding her with the mighty Sword of State. Like many a child at its christening, Mary cried through-out the entire ceremony!

THE PALACE IN

STIRLING CASTLE

RISING UP BEHIND

THE FOREWORK.

THE CHAPEL ROYAL

LAY BEYOND THE

PALACE

THE BIRTHCHAMBER
OF PRINCE JAMES IN
EDINBURGH CASTLE

STIRLING CASTLE, GUARDING THE
FIRST FORDABLE POINT ON THE RIVER FORTH.
STIRLING CASTLE, THE "BROOCH" HOLDING
SCOTLAND TOGETHER.
KING JAMES III "TUIK SIC PLESOUR TO DWELL
THAIR BECAUSE HE THOCHT IT (THE) MAIST
PLEASENTEST DWELLING".

THE KIRK
OF THE
HOLY RUDE,
STIRLING

QUEEN MARY AND PRINCE JAMES

At the age of five, Mary was sent to France for safety. There she married the Dauphin, became Queen of France and was widowed - all by the time she was eighteen. While in France Mary received the Golden Rose from Pope Pius IV in 1560, the fourth Scottish monarch to be so honoured.

In the following year Mary returned to Scotland and, in 1565, married Henry, Lord Darnley. She bore him a son, James Charles, on 19 June 1566, in a small room within the Palace in Edinburgh Castle. Straightaway the young babe was taken from his mother's arms and carried to Stirling Castle. Within a year of the Prince's birth, his father Darnley had been murdered, his mother Mary had remarried and been forced to abdicate in favour of her son. In May 1568 she fled the country never to return. In her Letters of Abdication, Queen Mary wrote:

> "nothing earthly can be more comfortable and happy to Us in this earth, than in Our lifetime to see Our most dear son, the native Prince of this Our Realm placed in the Kingdom thereof, and the Crown Royal set upon his head."

For the third time in a century the new monarch of Scotland was an infant. King James VI was crowned at Stirling on 29 July 1567, in the Kirk of the Holy Rude. The Crown, Sword and Sceptre, brought from Edinburgh Castle for the occasion, were placed briefly upon the thirteen-month-old child and returned to Edinburgh immediately afterwards.

THE COMMEMORATIVE PLAQUE

IN EDINBURGH CASTLE TO

SIR WILLIAM KIRKCALDY

OF GRANGE

THE HONOURS AND THE "LANG SIEGE"

The Keeper of Edinburgh Castle who had authorised the despatch of the Honours to Stirling was James Balfour of Pittendreich. Not long after, he was replaced as Keeper by Sir William Kirkcaldy of Grange, who was charged by the Regent, the Earl of Moray (the deposed Queen's half-brother), to maintain the "principal strength of the Realm" on behalf of the infant King. Mary still had some supporters fighting on her behalf and by 1571 Sir William Kirkcaldy had become one of them, possibly because his patron, the Regent, had been assassinated. Kirkcaldy now steadfastly held the Castle on behalf of his exiled Queen and resolutely refused to let the Honours be used by the new Regent, the Earl of Lennox, and his supporting group of nobles.

THE ASSAULT ON

EDINBURGH CASTLE,

MAY 1573

A SESSION OF THE SCOTTISH
PARLIAMENT. THE HONOURS ARE
ON THE TABLE IN FRONT OF THE
CANOPIED THRONE

By this time the Crown, Sword and Sceptre had acquired an additional role to that of Coronation Regalia. They symbolised the royal presence at meetings of the Parliament, adding to the panoply of majesty, particularly when an infant sovereign could not be present. The Honours were laid on a table before the monarch's place whenever Parliament met. An Act of Parliament became law only when the King, or his Commissioners, took up the Sceptre and used it to touch the relevant document.

Because the Honours were not obtainable for a meeting of the Parliament to be held in Stirling during late August 1571, the Regent devised alternatives. On 17 August an Edinburgh goldsmith, Mungo Bradie, was given 1lb of silver to manufacture a crown of honour and a sceptre. Bradie also received 6 gold coins and 12ozs of mercury to gild the pieces. A sword with a silver-gilt hilt was supplied by a cutler.

The substitute honours were transported from Leith by ship across the Forth to Burntisland where two horses were hired to carry them and Mungo Bradie to Stirling in time for the meeting. These substitutes were again used at a meeting of Parliament held in Edinburgh during April 1573.

By now Sir William Kirkcaldy had been holding the Castle for Queen Mary for almost two years. The siege of the Castle had begun in earnest in the Summer of 1571 and had continued in a desultory fashion since. Only after a devastating bombardment in May 1573 did the gallant Kirkcaldy surrender and the Castle fall to the King's party. Not for nothing was it called the "Lang Siege". While Kirkcaldy was paying for his loyalty to Mary with his life, the substitute honours were probably being melted down leaving the real Honours to take their place once more in the life of Royal Scotland.

SCOTLAND'S "SECOND KING"

From the reign of King James VI, the Crown of Scotland was used to crown a "second king". Records from the end of the fourteenth century show there were two Kings of Scotland. One was the legitimate monarch of the Scots, the other was the Lord Lyon King of Arms, the royal officer who granted coats of arms to deserving persons on behalf of the sovereign. His official title is derived from the main charge on the Royal Arms of Scotland, a rampant lion.

In 1592 King James appointed David Lindsay of the Mount Secundus as his King of Arms. At Stirling Castle on Saturday 27 May, David Lindsay was knighted by the King and the following day in the Chapel Royal he was crowned by his sovereign with the Crown of Scotland and presented with a baton of office. After the ceremony Sir David, wearing the Crown, dined at the same table as the King.

Twenty-nine years later, on Sunday 17 June 1621, Sir David's successor was installed as King of Arms during a ceremony held in the Palace of Holyroodhouse. The new Lord Lyon was Sir David's son-in-law, Sir Jerome Lindsay. In the King's absence, he was knighted by the Lord High Chancellor of Scotland, the Earl of Dunfermline, who then placed the Crown of Scotland on the head of the new King of Arms.

Subsequent Lord Lyons were installed in much the same fashion until Sir Charles Erskine of Cambo in 1681. By the time he died in 1727, the Honours of Scotland were no longer available for coronation ceremonies.

THE HONOURS AND THE UNION OF THE CROWNS

In 1578 King James VI's minority came to an end. He ruled Scotland for 25 years, until 1603, the year the unmarried Queen Elizabeth I of England died. James was her heir and he wasted no time in travelling to England to claim the rich throne and be crowned King James I of England.

James's departure had a profound effect on the significance of the Honours. Because the country now had an absent sovereign the symbols of majesty became a substitute. The aura gained by Crown, Sword and Sceptre after 1603 is part of the continuing respect with which they are regarded to this day. Scotland lost a resident King but gained potent alternatives. The Honours came to embody Scotland in a way which other European Crown Jewels do not, except perhaps the Crown of Hungary which is similarly regarded and respected as the life force of Hungarian nationhood.

NOBIS·HÆC·INVICTA
MISERVNT·106·PROAVI

One symbol of this respect was the popularity of the Honours as decorative devices. They had appeared on a coin struck in 1602; afterwards they were painted, carved in wood and stone and rendered in plaster. This respect was further demonstrated between 1615 and 1617, during the course of a major remodelling of the Palace in Edinburgh Castle in time for the "hamecoming" of King James to his ancient Kingdom. A room beside the King's private apartment was made ready to serve as a permanent repository for the Honours of Scotland. Stone-vaulted above and below, both for better security and as a precaution against fire, this was the very Crown Room in which the Honours are still stored and displayed.

Troubled

CHARLES, CANONS, COVENANTS - AND CROMWELL

KING JAMES VI

CHARLES,
DUKE OF
ALBANY

On 27 March 1625, the "blessed King James" passed away. His reign had been relatively peaceful. "Here I sit", he wrote, "and govern Scotland with my pen... which others could not govern by the sword".

King James's younger son, Charles, Duke of Albany, succeeded to the throne as King Charles I. Although born in Scotland, at Dunfermline Palace on 19 November 1600, Charles was brought up in London and was apt at times to treat his fellow countrymen with disdain. Since the Union of the Crowns of Scotland and England in 1603, the very personal kingship of the Kings of Scots had been replaced by an absentee monarchy. The situation called for wisdom and prudence on the part of the king. King James possessed such pragmatism and diplomacy; King Charles did not, with the direst of consequences both for the King and for his country. The Honours of Scotland, the paramount symbols of kingly power, were inevitably caught up in the troubled times that followed.

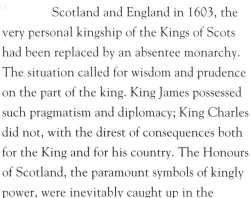

ABOVE

THE EXECUTION
OF KING CHARLES I,
30 JANUARY 1649

RIGHT

THE ABBEY AND
PALACE OF
HOLYROODHOUSE IN
THE SEVENTEENTH
CENTURY

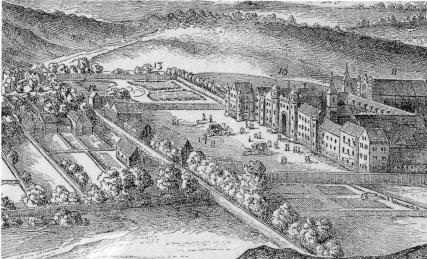

Times

THE CORONATION OF KING CHARLES I

Soon after Charles's accession, plans were made for the King's return to his native land for his Coronation as King of Scots. Rumours circulated that he was to come in 1626, but he never appeared. In 1628, and again in 1631, costly preparations were put in hand, but still His Majesty did not return. Eventually Charles did return, in June 1633, to great rejoicing and amid the most elaborate celebrations. The central event of the King's visit was his Coronation, which took place on 18 June at the Palace of Holyroodhouse in Edinburgh. The ceremony was one of great pomp and solemnity.

The King spent the night before his Coronation in Edinburgh Castle, the last monarch to sleep in the principal royal castle of Scotland. On the following morning, suitably robed and accompanied by the Great Chamberlain, the Lord High Constable, the Earl Marischal and a host of others, he made his way on horseback down the Royal Mile to Holyrood. Before him in the procession were carried the Honours of Scotland: the Spurs borne by the Earl of Eglinton, the Sword of State by the Earl of Buchan, the Sceptre by the Earl of Rothes, and finally the Crown itself borne by the Marquis of Douglas.

The ceremony in the Chapel Royal, the old abbey church beside the Palace, was both lengthy and solemn. For the first part of the service the Honours lay on a little table covered with green velvet laced and fringed with gold and placed close by the communion table. Following the sermon Archbishop Spottiswoode of St Andrews formally presented Charles to

his people and anointed him King. Then the Coronation proper began.

Firstly the Great Chamberlain mantled the King with the "Robe Royall", once worn by his great-grandfather King James IV. Then the Sword was girded round the King's waist by the Great Constable, and the Spurs put on his feet by the Earl Marischal. Taking the Crown,

the Archbishop placed it upon the King's head. Next the Lord Lyon King of Arms proclaimed the new monarch of Scotland's titles before the senior nobility took the oath of allegiance. Following this the Sword was removed from the King by the Great Chamberlain, and placed upon the communion table by the Archbishop, who then placed the Sceptre in the King's right hand and enthroned him. Thereafter the remainder of the nobility and the senior clergy paid homage to their new King. At the end of the ceremony the King returned to his state apartments in the Palace mantled, crowned and carrying the Sceptre. The cannon in the castle fired salvoes in his honour.

It was "canons" of a quite different sort which contributed to King Charles's eventual downfall. These were the Canons of ecclesiastical law issued in 1636. The King's Scottish subjects greatly resented his tampering with the religious life of the nation. As the Bishop of London wrote at the time, the Canons would "make more noise than all the cannons in Edinburgh Castle". He was proved right. The Scots rose up in revolt against their King and signed the National Covenant of protest.

With Edinburgh in the grip of
Covenanting fever, the Honours were taken
secretly from the Castle and removed to
Dalkeith Castle for safe-keeping. There they
remained until April 1639, when the garrison
was forced to surrender to the Covenanters.
The "royall ornamentis" were returned to
Edinburgh Castle, also by now held by the
Covenanters. The King was powerless to
intervene. Having got as far as Berwick-upon-
Tweed at the head of a reluctant English force,
he was prevented from entering Scotland by
General Leslie's Covenanting army encamped
on Duns Law.

The consequences of this first "Bishops'
War" were momentous not only for the
Kingdom of Scotland but for two of Charles's
other three kingdoms also. In 1641 Ireland was
in revolt and by August 1642 England too.
The consequences for the King himself were
fatal. After surrendering to the Scots in May
1646, he was handed over to the English on
30 January 1647. Exactly two years later,
the King was beheaded on the orders of
Oliver Cromwell.

THE CORONATION OF KING CHARLES II

The beheading of King Charles I came
as a great shock to the Scots. They may have
profoundly disagreed with their King, but they
had no desire to sweep away the monarchy.
Within a few days of the King's execution,
Parliament had proclaimed his son Charles II,
King of Scotland. In June the following year
King Charles entered his northern kingdom.

Cromwell, outraged, invaded Scotland.
On 3 September 1650 his New Model Army
inflicted a humiliating defeat on Leslie's
superior forces at Dunbar in East Lothian and
threatened to advance on Edinburgh. The
King, who had yet to be crowned, as well as the
Honours of Scotland, were in grave danger.

ABOVE

OLIVER CROMWELL AT THE

BATTLE OF DUNBAR, 1650

BELOW

THE CORONATION OF KING CHARLES II

AT SCONE, 1 JANUARY 1651

Straightaway the Honours were removed from Edinburgh Castle and taken north, perhaps to the safety of another mighty royal castle, Stirling. At the same time preparations were made for the Coronation of the new King. On 1 January 1651, in the tiny church atop the Moot Hill at Scone, King Charles II was enthroned. It proved to be the last Coronation to take place in Scotland.

Despite the great haste, the ceremony was conducted with due pomp and solemnity. Though not so grand as that for his father, it was clearly just as lengthy. "The exhortatioun wes sumthing large", the chronicler wryly noted, a reference to the over-long sermon delivered by a leading Presbyterian minister. And just as before, the Honours took their place in the proceedings.

Curiously, one feature of his father's Coronation at Holyrood was omitted, and another added. King Charles II was not anointed, because it was regarded as a Popish ritual. The "new" feature was a return to a practice dating from earlier inaugurations of Kings of Scots. The enthronement ceremony ended with the reading of the King's genealogy back to the legendary Fergus I.

KING FERGUS I,
LEGENDARY ANCESTOR
OF KING CHARLES II

CROMWELL AND THE HONOURS

The Coronation of King Charles II over, the Honours could not be returned to the security of the Crown Room in Edinburgh Castle, for that fortress had fallen to Cromwell on Christmas Eve 1650. Indeed, the Protector's army was fast advancing on Scone. On 6 June 1651, on the last day of the Parliament held in Perth, the King ordained "the Erle of Marchell to cause transport the saidis Honouris to the hous of Dunnottor, thair to be keepit by him till farther ordouris".

The Earl Marischal, in fact, was lying a prisoner in the Tower of London, but his representatives carried out the King's instruction and spirited the Honours north-east to the Earl's castle at Dunnottar. The King meanwhile headed south-west with the Scottish army to England, to defeat at Worcester on 3 September and flight to France. His kingdom and his Honours were at the mercy of Cromwell.

OLIVER CROMWELL

Cromwell was determined to lay his hands on the Scottish Crown Jewels, to do what he had earlier done with those of England, – destroy them. His men, under the command of General Monck, took Perth on 2 August but found the cupboard bare. English intelligence suggested that the Honours had gone north-east. Monck followed in hot pursuit. Dundee was taken by storm on 1 September. Aberdonians, probably horrified by the reports coming from Dundee of 1,000 deaths, including 200 women and children, opened their gates to Monck's army and escaped with a £1,000 fine. By the end of September the English were before Dunnottar Castle in strength. Inside the fortress were just forty men, two sergeants, one lieutenant, their commanding officer, George Ogilvie of Barras, and the Honours of Scotland.

DUNNOTTAR
AND DEEDS OF
DERRING-DO

The story of how the defenders of
Dunnottar withstood the might of Cromwell's
army for eight bitter winter months; of how the
Honours were smuggled out from the castle
under the very noses of the English and hidden
beneath the floor of the nearby Kirk of Kinneff;
and of how they lay buried there for eight long
years until returned once more to Edinburgh
Castle, is one of the most well-kent, oft-repeated
tales of Scottish history.

No matter that there are greatly conflict-
ing accounts as to how, precisely, the Honours
were removed. The most important thing for
Scots, then and today, is that the Honours were
preserved for posterity. The Lord Chancellor
of the day, the Earl of Loudoun, spoke of
"an inexpressible loss and shame if these thingis
(meaning the Honours) shall be taken by the
enemie". He spoke for the entire nation. And
we today owe an enormous debt to those men
and women who gave their lives, or risked
doing so, in the preservation of the Honours
of Scotland. For without their courage, visitors
to the Crown Room in Edinburgh Castle today
would not be able to gaze in wonderment
before the oldest set of sovereign regalia in the
British Isles.

One account of the smuggling out of
the Honours tells of them being lowered over
the walls of the castle on the seaward side,
where they were received by a serving woman
pretending to gather seaweed. She carried them
off, safely concealed in her creel, to the parish
kirk at Kinneff where they were buried beneath
the floor.

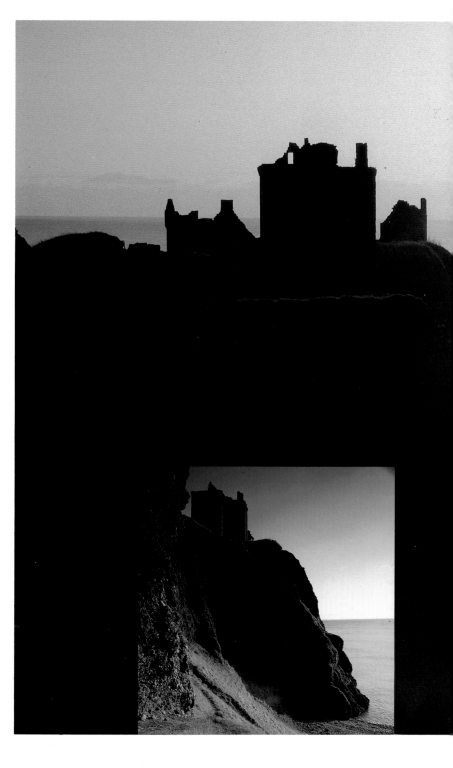

DUNNOTTAR, UPON ITS ISOLATED ROCKY PERCH,
THRUSTING OUT FROM THE PRECIPITOUS KINCARDINESHIRE COAST INTO
THE CHILLY WATERS OF THE NORTH SEA.
DUNNOTTAR, ANCIENT STRONGHOLD OF THE KEITH FAMILY,
AND CHIEF SEAT OF THE POWERFUL EARL MARISCHALS OF SCOTLAND.

"TO HIM WHO IS FAMILIAR WITH ITS STORY,
DUNNOTTAR SPEAKS WITH AN AUDIBLE VOICE;
EVERY CAVE HAS A RECORD, EVERY TURRET A TONGUE;
HIS EAR IS STRUCK WITH WANDERING VOICES;
AND THE WORDS THAT NEVER DIE SEEM
AT EVERY STEP TO ARREST HIS ATTENTION."

(W. BEATTIE CALEDONIA ILLUSTRATED)

The more popular, and certainly more thrilling, account has Christian Granger, the minister of Kinneff's wife, and her serving-woman as the heroines of the piece. Mrs Granger had obtained leave from the English commander, Colonel Morgan, to enter the castle, on the pretext of visiting the Governor's wife. While there, the Honours were entrusted to her, and boldly taken out of the castle, the Crown and Sceptre concealed under her clothes, and the much lengthier Sword and Scabbard in bundles of flax carried by her servant. Legend has it that the breaks visible in both the sword blade and scabbard are a result of the serving-woman attempting to make the concealment more effective. Together they passed through the English camp without suspicion. On reaching her horse, Mrs Granger was temporarily thrown into a panic when the Colonel politely assisted her to mount. His suspicions were not aroused and the two women, with the Honours, were safe - for the moment.

The Honours were hidden first, it is said, at the bottom of the bed in the manse until the minister could bury them more securely in the kirk. "For the Crown and Sceptre", he later wrote to the Countess Marischal, "I raised the pavement-stone just before the pulpit, in the night tyme, and digged under it ane hole, and put them in there, and filled up the hole, and layed down the stone just as it was before, and removed the mould that remained, that none would have discerned the stone to have been raised at all. The Sword again, at the west end of the church, amongst some common saits (pews) that stand there, I digged down in the ground betwixt the twa foremost, and laid it doun without the case (scabbard) of it, and covered it up".

On 26 May 1652, the long siege of Dunnottar Castle finally ended. It was the last stronghold to fall to the English. Cromwell was clearly still confident that the Scottish Regalia were within his grasp for one of the articles of capitulation of the garrison provided "that the Croun and Scepter of Scotland, together with all other ensigns of Regallitie, be delivered to mee". He was to be bitterly disappointed once again. Angry and frustrated, Cromwell's men plundered the castle of its remaining treasures while the governor and his lady were harshly imprisoned. Neither would give up their secret, however, and though George Ogilvie lived to tell the tale, his wife died from the effects of her treatment.

While Cromwell held sway over Scotland, the Honours were never safe. Every now and then, Mr and Mrs Granger went to the kirk at the dead of night to lift the Honours out from their hiding-places and make sure that all was well.

Gradually the threat from the English troops billeted nearby faded, possibly because of a growing rumour that the Honours had been smuggled out of the castle, over the sea to France.

Cromwell died in 1658. Two years later, on 14 May 1660, in Edinburgh, King Charles II was proclaimed King of three kingdoms. As the Honours were returned to Edinburgh Castle, the cannon fired in salute. The sovereign was overjoyed and in a letter dated 4 September of that year wrote to the Countess Marischal:

One item of Regalia was not smuggled
out to Kinneff Kirk but was retained by George
Ogilvie as a memento - the elaborate Sword
Belt. In 1790 it was accidentally discovered
built into a garden wall at his house at Barras.
It was returned by a descendant of his to
its rightful place in the Crown Room in
Edinburgh Castle in 1892.

THE SWORD BELT,
SEPARATED FROM
THE HONOURS
FOR 242 YEARS

KINNEFF KIRK AND MANSE, 10 MILES
SOUTH OF DUNNOTTAR CASTLE.
THE PRESENT CHURCH STANDS ON THE
SITE OF THE REVEREND GRANGER'S KIRK

ROYAL GRATITUDE

An unique heraldic method of expressing
thanks was used by King Charles II following his
Restoration to reward two of the men involved in
preserving the Honours of Scotland from the hands
of Cromwell. Each man was given an augmentation,
or addition, to his coat of arms which alluded to
the Honours of Scotland and the Royal House
of Scotland.

John Keith, son of the Earl Marischal, was
granted an augmentation of Gules a sceptre and
sword in saltire with an imperial crown in chief,
within an orle (border) of eight thistles Or. He was
also made Knight Marischal of Scotland and created,
seventeen years later, Earl of Kintore, Lord Keith
of Inverurie and Keith Hall.

George Ogilvie of Barras, whose wife died
in prison after the taking of Dunnottar Castle, was
granted the addition of a crowned thistle to his coat
of arms. This is the Royal Plant Badge of Scotland,
first used by King James V and still employed by
Her Majesty The Queen in Scotland. Ogilvie of
Barras also became a Knight Baronet and as
Sir George Ogilvie of Barras his armorial ensigns
carried the Arms of Nova Scotia on a canton.

These royal marks of gratitude became part
of the Arms of Kintore and Ogilvie and have been
enjoyed by their descendants ever since.

THE HONOURS AND THE "SITTING DOWN" OF PARLIAMENT

After 1651, the Honours were never again used to crown a sovereign. Their principal use was now at sittings of the Parliament in Edinburgh. They served to signify the King's presence now that he chose not to visit his northern kingdom. More than ever before, perhaps, these symbols of sovereignty were treated by the nation with a reverence not witnessed while her monarch reigned in person.

From the first meeting of Parliament after the King's Restoration, which sat in January 1661, to the last of all, which was adjourned in March 1707, the Honours were taken in procession out from the Crown Room in the Castle and down to Parliament House in the Royal Mile. There they lay, centre stage, signifying the sovereign's presence, and at the passing of each act the sovereign's consent was signified by the touching of the Sceptre upon the parchment.

The carriage of the Honours to Parliament, and their transport back again, was carried out with great ceremony. By the late seventeenth century it had come to be called the "Ryding of the Parliament". It was a most elaborate procession, not unlike that for Coronations. The representatives of the Three Estates (the clergy, nobility and burgesses) walked before the senior Officers of State. Immediately behind the Lyon King of Arms came the Crown, Sceptre and Sword, in that order, borne by the appropriate dignitaries and attended by Heralds and Pursuivants. Throughout the progress, trumpets sounded and cannons roared from the battlements of the Castle.

THE HONOURS AND THE UNION OF THE PARLIAMENTS

When Parliament assembled on 3 October 1706 it proved to be for the last time. With the Honours in their accustomed place in Parliament House, the members debated long and hard on the matter in hand - union with England. At last, on 16 January 1707, the Treaty of Union was formally ratified and the Lord Chancellor, the Earl of Seafield, touched the Act with the Sceptre. Handing it back to the clerk, Chancellor Seafield uttered the immortal words: "Now, there's an end of an auld sang".

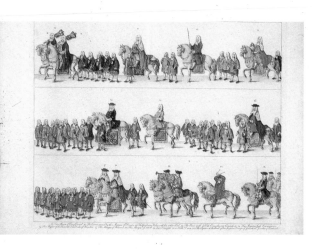

ARTICLE XXIV OF THE TREATY OF UNION BETWEEN THE KINGDOMS OF SCOTLAND AND

ENGLAND INCORPORATING THE REFERENCE TO THE HONOURS OF SCOTLAND

QUEEN ANNE

RECEIVING A COPY

OF THE ARTICLES OF

UNION FROM THE

COMMISSIONERS

The Treaty of Union, including the Article referring to the Honours of Scotland, was approved by the English Parliament on 19 March. Both Parliaments were now no more; a new United Kingdom Parliament would meet, in London, from now on.

The Scottish Parliament was adjourned on 26 March. The Honours were now deprived of all practical use, either as coronation insignia or as symbols of sovereignty at sittings of the Parliament. A farewell speech was composed for the Crown:

> *"I royal diadem relinquished stand*
> *By all my friends and robbed of my land*
> *So left bereft of all I did command…"*

The Honours were handed over to the Lord Treasurer-Depute and taken back up to the Castle. There, in the stone-vaulted Crown Room which had been built for them ninety years before, they were safely locked away in the great oak chest for another time. The openings into the vault were walled up and the Honours of Scotland, the symbols of sovereignty for more than two hundred years, were left in peace.

Of the twenty-five Articles of Union in the Treaty, one referred to the Honours themselves. During the heated debate great concern had been expressed that the Regalia might be carried off to London, never to return. Though many parts of the Treaty were the subject of intense discussion, not a single voice spoke out against the Article declaring:

"That the Croun, Sceptre,
and Sword of State…continue
to be kept as they are within that
part of the United Kingdom now
called Scotland; and that they
shall so remain in all times coming,
notwithstanding the Union."

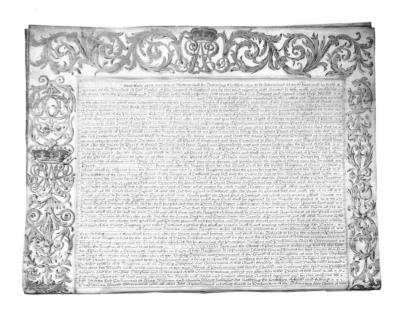

Lost and

The Honours lay entombed within the Crown Room in the Castle. In time, people began to question whether they had ever been placed there, and rumours circulated that they had been secretly removed to England in contravention of the Treaty of Union. There was even a report that the ancient Crown of Scotland had been shown in the Tower of London. The closed-up room in the Castle became something of a mystery to the soldiers serving in the garrison.

Eighty-seven years after the Honours had been locked away, on 5 November 1794, the Crown Room was briefly opened up by the Castle's Lieutenant-Governor, Major Drummond, who was searching for some lost Parliamentary records. In the darkened, dust-filled room he saw the great oak chest. He repeatedly shook it, but it returned no sound. With no authority from King George III to open the chest, he left the room and walled up the opening once more, more convinced than ever that the Honours were gone.

THE HONOURS OF SCOTLAND
ON DISPLAY SHORTLY AFTER
THEIR REDISCOVERY IN 1818

WALTER SCOTT
SHOWS OFF
THE HONOURS
OF SCOTLAND

THE HONOURS
OF SCOTLAND
ADVERTISED

Found

WALTER SCOTT
DISCOVERS
THE HONOURS

CROWN SQUARE IN EDINBURGH
CASTLE, ABOUT 1819. THE HEAVILY
GRILLED WINDOW TO THE RIGHT OF
THE STAIR TOWER MARKS THE
POSITION OF THE CROWN ROOM.
THE TOP TWO STOREYS OF THE STAIR
TOWER WERE ADDED SHORTLY AFTER
THE REDISCOVERY OF THE HONOURS
OF SCOTLAND IN 1818.

The anxiety felt by Major Drummond in 1794 about the fate of the Honours was shared by Walter Scott and the Officers of State with him as, twenty-four years later, they gathered on the steps outside the Crown Room. They were ready to unblock the doorway once more and this time, armed with the Royal Warrant, to force open the lid of the great oak chest. As the workmen set to their task, Scott later wrote, "the general impression that the Regalia had been secretly removed weighed heavily on the hearts of all".

Their fears were unfounded. As the lid of the chest creaked open, there lay the Crown, Sword and Sceptre precisely as they had been left in 1707. As the glinting Honours of Scotland emerged from their linen wrappings, Walter Scott and those with him in the Crown Room were overwhelmed by uncontrollable joy. The news travelled fast and soon the people of Scotland were rejoicing at the rediscovery.

Preparations were now put in hand for the permanent display of the Honours in the Crown Room which had been their home since 1617. A second Royal Warrant, issued on 8 July 1818, appointed the Keeper of the Great Seal of Scotland, the Keeper of the Privy Seal, His Majesty's Advocate, the Lord Clerk Register, and the Lord Justice Clerk to be Commissioners for the Keeping of the Regalia.

Their first task was to appoint Sir Adam Ferguson, a friend of Walter Scott, Keeper of the Regalia and to give him a flat in the Palace directly above the Crown Room.

The public were now invited to inspect the Honours for themselves. In 1819 folk were charged the princely sum of one shilling each (at least £7.50 at 1993 prices!) just for the privilege of viewing them. There they have remained ever since.

47

KING GEORGE IV
RECEIVES
THE HONOURS

In 1821 the Prince Regent, who had
granted the Royal Warrant leading to their
rediscovery, was crowned King George IV.
The following year he paid the first royal visit
to Scotland by a reigning sovereign since
that of King Charles II in 1651.

The visit was stage-managed by Walter
Scott and on Monday 12 August, shortly before
the King's arrival at Leith, the Honours were
conveyed in great procession from the Castle
by the Knight Marischal, escorted by a troop of
Highlanders, to the Palace of Holyroodhouse.
They were to remain there for the duration of
the King's stay and so "grace the presence of
the King". The *Edinburgh Evening Courant*
reported that "the pavements of the streets and
the windows and balconies, in front of which
the procession passed, were crowded with a
brilliant association of beauty and fashion."

Such was the enthusiasm of the
Edinburgh public both for the newly-
discovered Honours and their recently arrived
King that among the attractions laid on for the
visit was a large representation of an imperial
crown, erected on the top of one of the flues at
the gas works, which when illuminated at night
"had a beautiful effect"!

On arriving at the Palace of
Holyroodhouse on 15 August, His Majesty
formally received the Crown, Sceptre and
Sword of State from the Duke of Hamilton,
Lord Francis Leveson Gower (representing the
Earl of Sutherland) and the Earl of Errol
respectively. In touching each emblem, he
realised his kingship of the nation.

One week later, the King's tour
culminated in a grand procession to restore
the Honours to the Castle. It was a dreich
summer's day but the weather did nothing to
dampen the enthusiasm either of the huge
crowds that lined the route or of the King
himself.

MONARCH AND

REGALIA REUNITED

AFTER 171 YEARS

The King "stood upon the summit of
Edina's grey crest" and bade the Honours farewell
and they were returned to the Crown Room.

The Honours did not leave the Castle
again for another 132 years. They did, however,
leave the Crown Room.

BURIED ONCE MORE!

The Honours were buried not once but twice in their eventful history. In 1651 they had been concealed from Cromwell; in 1939 they were hidden once more to prevent them from falling into German hands.

At the outbreak of the War the Honours were packed into the great oak chest and taken down to a cellar beneath the Crown Room and covered with sand bags. The worry at that time was the risk of damage from aerial bombardment. But as the War progressed, concern mounted about the likelihood of a German invasion and the possibility of the Honours falling into enemy hands. More serious measures were called for.

On 12 May 1941 the Honours were taken out from the chest, packed into two zinc-lined cases and buried in separate locations in the ruins of David's Tower, the medieval tower house entombed beneath the Half-Moon Battery close by the Palace. The Crown and the Stewart Jewels were buried beneath the floor of a latrine-closet, the Sceptre, Sword of State, Belt, Scabbard and Wand were concealed in a wall. Plans indicating the locations were sealed in envelopes and sent in the utmost secrecy, one each to His Majesty King George VI, The Secretary of State for Scotland, The King's and Lords' Treasurer's Remembrancer and the Governor General of Canada.

When the War ended in victory the Honours were restored once more to public display.

THE NATIONAL SERVICE OF THANKSGIVING, 1953

On Wednesday 24 June 1953, the Honours were taken from the Castle by the Lord Lyon King of Arms and his brother Heralds, escorted by The Queen's Bodyguard for Scotland, The Royal Company of Archers, who marched on each side of an open carriage bearing the Officers. Lord Lyon held the Crown, Rothesay Herald carried the Sword of State upright and Marchmont Herald cradled the Sceptre on his right arm. All were bare-headed out of respect for the precious burdens in their care.

The destination for the Honours was the High Kirk of St Giles, in Edinburgh's High Street, where a National Service of Thanksgiving took place in the presence of the new Sovereign, Queen Elizabeth. The Honours were carried to the Holy Table where they lay throughout the ensuing act of worship. The climax came at the close of the service when the Minister of St Giles lifted the Sceptre of Scotland from the Table, presented it to Her Majesty who in turn handed it to the Earl of Crawford and Balcarres. She next received the Sword of State before placing it in the care of the Earl of Home. Finally the Minister took the Crown of Scotland on its cushion from the Holy Table and offered it to the Sovereign who took its weight before giving it to the Duke of Hamilton who was on bended knee. Thereafter, preceded by Her Honours, The Queen and Duke of Edinburgh walked through the congregation to be greeted by the citizens of Edinburgh who acclaimed the Sovereign outside the High Kirk.

THE SWORD OF STATE
AND
THE ORDER OF THE THISTLE

The National Service in St Giles in the summer of 1953 was the first occasion the Honours had been taken from the Castle since 1822, but the Sword of State, alone, had been taken out forty-two years earlier, also to St Giles.

On Wednesday 19 July 1911 His Majesty King George V inaugurated the newly-built Chapel of the Order of the Thistle. The Sword of State was carried in front of the King on that occasion.

The link between the Sword of State and the Order of the Thistle was not re-established until 1971 when the Sword was part of the ceremonial involved in the Installation of a Knight of the Most Ancient and Most Noble Order of the Thistle, Scotland's premier Order of Chivalry.

The Sword was present on all subsequent installations until 1987, the tercentenary anniversary of the Order.

Additions to

Since 1818, the Honours of Scotland have been joined on display by other precious royal jewels. They are described here.

THE WAND

Walter Scott discovered a fourth object in the oak chest alongside the Crown, Sword of State and Sceptre - a silver-gilt wand. What its function was, and why it was in the chest at all, have never been satisfactorily answered.

The wand, 1 metre long, is topped by an oval-faceted globe of rock crystal surmounted by a cross. The wand can be separated into three pieces. The finial unscrews and the rod pulls apart in two sections. These bear the unknown maker's mark F G. The rod is reinforced by a wooden core.

The exact purpose of the wand is unknown. Sir Walter Scott suggested that it might have been carried before the Lord High Treasurer of Scotland. Records from 1616 mention a Lord Treasurer's Mace but this would have been a different shape with a bulbous head surmounted by arches having an orb and cross finial.

PRINCE HENRY,

CARDINAL YORK

THE STEWART JEWELS

Four items are associated with the Royal House of Stewart.

The last male Stewart monarch to rule Scotland was King James VII, King Charles II's younger brother. Within four years of his Accession in 1685, he and his family were exiles in France. James took with him three pieces of personal insignia, and the Ring traditionally thought to have been worn by King Charles I at his English Coronation in 1625.

James bequeathed the Stewart Jewels to his son, Prince James Francis Edward, the "Old Pretender", who in turn left them to his elder son, Prince Charles Edward, "Bonnie Prince Charlie". When he died in 1788 without an heir, the Jewels passed to his younger brother, Prince Henry.

Henry's character was quite different from his elder brother. Born in 1725 he made the Church of Rome his career. He was created a Cardinal in 1747 and used the title Cardinal York.

When Napoleon Bonaparte invaded the Papal States in 1796 Cardinal York became a refugee. He joined the King and Queen of the Two Sicilies, and from there he travelled to Venice where he remained in extreme poverty. Despite this he was never tempted to sell the Stewart Jewels.

A remarkable gesture relieved the Cardinal's financial problems. King George III, Protestant ruler of Britain, learned of the plight of the last Stewart claimant to his throne and arranged for a handsome annuity to be paid to Cardinal York.

THE ST ANDREW

JEWEL OF THE OR

OF THE THISTLE

The Honours

When the Cardinal died in 1807 he left the Stewart Jewels to King George III. Thus they returned to Great Britain after an absence of one hundred and nineteen years. By the express command of King William IV the Jewels were returned to Scotland where they were deposited in Edinburgh Castle on 18 December 1830.

THE ST ANDREW JEWEL OF THE ORDER OF THE THISTLE

The Jewel consists of an oval chalcedony cut with a cameo of St Andrew and his cross with a thistle below the figure. The cameo is surrounded by twelve large rose-cut diamonds with a larger diamond set on the ribbon loop. The original colour of the ribbon was dark purple. On the reverse is an enamelled oval circumscribed by the motto of the Order, NEMO ME IMPUNE LACESSIT ("No one assails me with impunity") in gold letters. The centre of the oval, bearing an enamelled thistle, is hinged and opens to reveal a miniature portrait of Princess Louise of Stolberg, wife of Bonnie Prince Charlie. Probably the original miniature showed Mary of Modena, first wife of King James VII. The Jewel bears no internal marks but was made by a London goldsmith between May 1687 and December 1688.

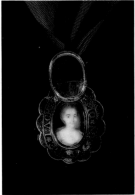

RIGHT   FAR RIGHT

THE REVERSE OF THE   THE CONCEALED MINIATURE

ST ANDREW JEWEL   WITHIN THE JEWEL

THE COLLAR OF THE ORDER
OF THE GARTER

This is of gold and enamel forming twenty-one garters containing a red rose. The garters are enamelled blue with gold letters giving the motto of the Order, HONI SOIT QUI MAL Y PENSE ("The shame be his who thinks ill of it"). The garter links alternate with double gold knots in the fashion of a cord with four tassel ends. The Collar measures 1562mm in length and weighs 33ozs 10dwt.

THE GREAT GEORGE OF THE
ORDER OF THE GARTER

This is named to distinguish it from the Lesser George, a gold badge which hangs on the blue riband of the Order. It is of gold and enamel in the form of St George on horseback slaying the dragon with a spear. The obverse of the George and its suspension link are studded with sixty-four rose-cut and fifty-seven table-cut diamonds. One table- and three rose-cut diamonds are missing. The reverse of the George is fully enamelled in colour. It is 72mm high by 65mm wide and bears no hallmark.

Both Collar and Great George may be of French workmanship and were probably made for King James VII.

THE COLLAR AND GREAT GEORGE OF THE ORDER OF THE GARTER

THE RUBY RING

THE RUBY RING

This was the final item bequeathed by Cardinal York. In its centre is a large, but very thin ruby, engraved with the cross of St George and foiled behind to provide additional depth of colour. The ruby is surrounded by twenty-six small diamonds set in silver. The head of the Ring is polished gold with engraved scroll work immediately next to the diamonds. The shoulders of the Ring are also engraved. The shank can be adjusted to fit fingers of all sizes.

THE ENAMELLED REVERSE OF THE GREAT GEORGE

THE LORNE JEWELS

A necklace, locket and pendant were bequeathed to the people of Scotland in 1939 by Princess Louise, the fourth daughter of Queen Victoria. She had received the London-made jewels on 23 August 1871 as a gift from the Clan Campbell to celebrate her marriage to John Campbell, Marquis of Lorne, later the 9th Duke of Argyll.

THE MARRIAGE OF LORD LORNE TO PRINCESS LOUISE, 1871

THE NECKLACE

The necklace is made of thirteen rectangles, set with a total of one hundred and ninety diamonds, connected by thirteen pearls encircled with diamonds.

THE LOCKET

This consists of a large oriental pearl surrounded by a row of ten rose diamonds with an outer row of ten smaller diamonds which alternate with ten lozenge-shaped diamonds.

THE PENDANT

The final part of the Jewel, a pear-shaped pendant, is attached to the locket by a double sprig of Bog Myrtle, the Campbell plant badge, formed of emeralds. On the pendant is a representation of the Galley of Lorne in relief. This is composed of sapphires on a pavé of diamonds. The Galley is surrounded with the motto of the Duke of Argyll, NE OBLIVISCARIS ("Do not forget") with letters set in diamond chips.

THE HONOURS OF
SCOTLAND, DISPLAYED
ON THE STAINED GLASS
IN THE GREAT HALL OF
EDINBURGH CASTLE

The book was designed by James Gardiner,
of James Gardiner Associates, Carrington, Midlothian,
and printed in Scotland by Nimmos of Edinburgh
on Consort Royal Silk paper manufactured by
The Donside Paper Company Limited, Aberdeen

First published in 1993 by

HISTORIC SCOTLAND

20 BRANDON STREET

EDINBURGH

EH3 5RA

ISBN 0 7480 0626 5

SILVER CAP BADGE OF

THE WARDEN OF REGALIA,

MADE IN EDINBURGH BY

MR JAMESON, GOLDSMITH,

IN 1960

Acknowledgements

In the preparation of this book, valued assistance has been
received from the following:

Patrick Cadell, keeper of the records of Scotland,
    Andrew Broom, deputy keeper, and Linda Ramsay,
    conservator, of the Scottish Record Office.
Alan Cameron, archivist, and staff at the Bank of Scotland.
Professor (Emeritus) Gordon Donaldson CBE,
    H.M. Historiographer in Scotland.
Elizabeth Fox, copy editor.
Jenny Hess, marketing manager, Historic Scotland.
Yvonne Holton, silversmith.
Brian Jackson, Department of Geology, National Museums
    of Scotland.
William Jameson BEM, goldsmith.
Gordon Lyall Associates, exhibition designers.
Duncan Macniven, deputy director, Historic Scotland.
The Earl and Countess of Mansfield, Scone Palace.
William Murray, Warden of Regalia.
Lady Ogilvy, Winton House.
Mrs C.G.W. Roads MVO, lyon clerk and keeper of records.
Joe White, photographic librarian, Historic Scotland.
Lieutenant-Colonel Donald Wickes MVO, superintendent
    of the Palace of Holyroodhouse.